G000162525

Also by Dominic Leonard

love, bring myself (Broken Sleep Books, 2019)

Glib & Oil (Legitimate Snack, 2020)

Dirt

Leonard

© 2021 Dominic Leonard. All rights reserved; no part of this book may be reproduced by any means without the publisher's permission.

ISBN: 978-1-913642-72-3

The author/s has asserted their right to be identified as the author of this Work in accordance with the Copyright, Designs and Patents Act 1988

Cover designed by Aaron Kent

Edited and typeset by Aaron Kent

Broken Sleep Books Ltd
Rhydwen,
Talgarreg,
SA44 4HB
Wales

Contents

Haruspex 9

Against Lustre 10

Dollhouse 11

I Fear Thunder & Lightning beyond Measure; But By
God's Head I Fear You more than All the Thunder &
Lightning in the World 12

Enemy of the People 13

Ape of Form 15

What is the wind, what is it 16

No Dark Pastoral 17

Revolt 18

A motorway is a very strong wind 19

And are the nudes, at the same time, closely related to
the appearance of specific people? Are they to some
extent portraits of bodies? 22

Whether Mortal Men May Attain True Happiness 23

Death Poem 24

Aubade 25

This Mysterious 26

Mary and the Angel 27

Landscape 28

Iafnlengd 29

Victorine 30

And So We Invented The Wheel 31

On deleting a villanelle about my grandfather 32

O 33

Notes 37

Acknowledgements 39

for my brother

Dirt

Dominic Leonard

Stitch not great and deepe wounds,
for that it is in danger to shut in
the corrupt and peraduenture
venemous matter

Haruspex

When the wind outside came in and bent me
Into ridicule I remembered these fingers
And the fibrous art of divination – how to descend
Into the body's yolk, the slick harbours of fat,
Pools and avenues that received me richly
Into the butter of their wanting; standing
There among the fractals I was pale
As a seawall in snow. The less you know
About pain and its fabulous geometry
The more you can do with it. I was taken to
A carving desk and made complex, had organs
Exchanged for floodlands and nerve endings
Concealed in a pink film. To be worshipped

Is to be broken from without. What's a place
Where my hands will get done their filthy business
In peace? I have looked again into the glass
In the sink to see what will come, casting the
Whole numb history of frailty and strength
Upon this shore, upon this work I did with my
Hands. All the crunchy pathos of human closeness.
The mind will believe whatever the body tells it, so I
Climbed out from its sugary depths and the gaps
Full of jewels and scribble and re-angled light
Were sealed shut – and I was awake, by the window,
Carving my mouth open so that evil could not be made
Within. To get out all the slush, all the necessary dirt.

Against Lustre

Lying in bed watching headlights
Swing silver across the room,
How bad to get up and walk around
Naked (soothingly). 10pm wine-sad.
Tasteful modern light pulls at my
Sleep shirt: *what is worthy of a smile*
In day-to-day life? Being good doesn't
Matter, and locally produced jam
Doesn't matter, and sex doesn't matter.
I am determined that an explanation
Should be simple... why they do this,
The living. The contemporary moment!
The momentary contempt of it!
The soul splashing about in what the body
Is made of! It is so useless to live together
Melodramatically; one huge deliberate
Funfair, each of us stood trembling
Forests and Prussian blue,
Hands jammed and breaking in the cogs
Of the world. Summer stamps on us.
In a soft wind clouds sop up the earth
Like slices of bread through
Filthy water. Please, a few more
Beautiful ideas. Just like that.
Breathy like that. Do that again.

Dollhouse

There was a mother
who fell back,
assiduously. I'm
most people are
always worrying
it is so difficult;
the world or
the world is
not enough. No
one really is alive
more than I am
alive, secured
to the sot & thrall
of the hurling thing,
aloft on the bough
of me; the boy I'd
want to know
is a fraud, hurting
blue, as a star retains
its hidden crush –
his swallow
of dark, his frame of
burning, a lit hilltop fir –
o glory to the
ground where I can
make a locket of this
body, to keep it,
to be not here only.

I Fear Thunder & Lightning beyond Measure; But By God's Head I Fear You more than All the Thunder & Lightning in the World

Cataclysm
Past & night
Feverous; I,

Hot as a pig
In the dark
& doughy

Back room –
Smell of suet,
Smoke, salt – heaved

From the clearing
Of these my
Chamber walls by

You yawning your heart
Down,
Spit, you

Spit on the ground.
I & mine
Twitching

& harvest. Passed
Father
Mother me fierce

Enemy of the People

What miserable drones and traitors have I nourished and brought up in my household, who let their lord be treated with such shameful contempt by a low-born cleric?

cornered him with three others by the monastic cloister in canterbury cathedral on the twenty ninth of december 1170 & struck him down so the blood was white with the brain & the brain no less red from the blood for the king shot him with a semiautomatic assault rifle for the king poisoned him for the king stabbed him twenty three times for the king the blood was white for the king the brain red for the king did what i was told for the king cut his throat for the king held his head underwater and waited for the thrashing to stop for the king shot him with a high power sniper rifle from the top floor of a bank across the plaza for the king poisoned his pink cocktail at the new years eve party for the king & my country no history of violence but did what the king said for the king long history of domestic violence & sexually violent threats online & did what the king said for the king & my country blood was white & brain no less red for the king switched out his pills for cyanide for the king sent bombs to his house for the king strangled him with a necktie for speaking against my king for the king

snuck into his house and smothered him while he
slept for the king smashed a plant pot over his head
for the king turned his blood white with brain and
brain red with blood for the king hanged him in the
garage and framed it as a suicide for the king shot him
through the heart with an arrow for the king planted
explosives under his car for the king planted evidence
for the king forged evidence for the king struck
him down for the king struck him down for the king
who is here so vile that will not love his country
cornered him in canterbury cathedral and struck
him down so the blood was white with the brain &
the brain no less red from the blood & the brain from
the blood with the brain & the brain with the blood
was white & red & blood no less was the brain &
the blood the blood & the brain was red & white
& white was red the red the blood no less the blood
was red & white & red & white & red & white & blue

Ape of Form

So long
the hour adheres to my purpose:

to have known suffering
nebulously, kept our life bound

by the mutation
of dominion and great buildings

ossified, pedestals
illustriously decorated, and locked gates

and fire within.
I have not changed a great deal

has changed. My moody riverside kingdom
burnt, focal and flightless,

and its deft dead
and their cold, yabbering hearts.

What is the wind, what is it
after Gertrude Stein

An egg – lithe beast that could crack with any pressure,
That gets yellower towards its centre, that hangs between
The fingers. A ghost-vision, serenely bovine. Incubated,
Stratified. A correct language of where it was, where it
Went, how are we anchored by it. But, to wander with it –
How the wind knocks my ham-fisted breath from me,
Makes a pelt of it. And wedged is the wind, trickling
Into and out of all my little compartments and rooms,
A fawn in a field seen blurred through the rain at nearly
Seven in the evening after stumbling from the house.
Something to consider when deciding on materials to
Rebuild the world from after testing its capacity for grief,
Which is all this was.

No Dark Pastoral

the sunlight was
different then it
swayed in stalks
like beautiful
blinking sisters
cloaked round in
Eros Eros Eros
I laid the knots of
light down piece
by piece into a
circle there is no
mist-flown field
no great holy
pond of black winds
just the last juice
of March draining
off the board
all my dreams are
wearing bright ugly
waistcoats & it is
spring almost definitely

Revolt

The news gets worse with every birthday.
I'd like to have strong principles
But these days I'm lifeless as a wallet –
I stood too close to the parts of myself
I knew would ruin me and felt my half-life

Drop notch by notch, click clack.
I started misreading *deposits* for *despots*
In adverts on the tube, started having
Nightmares about justice and judges,
Clouds revolting, rain turned hugely outside

Of itself, my heart clattering all the while
Beneath my skin like a broken trolley,
Desperate to prove itself; I scarcely have
The energy anymore to enjoy crucial and
Timely art. My pain is smaller

Than I'd ever imagined. I'm not sadder
But I am crueller. I could fill letter
After letter with my newfound malice
(Which had a touch of something
Glamorous to it), enough to fill a ha-ha

But there's already plenty to be crying
About. And, after everything, it wasn't
The worst year. I still wasn't ready
To protect any one thing and as always
Had just the right amount of life left.

A motorway is a very strong wind

We remember it differently, I know, but in my version
You couldn't bear this green emergency for long. Ambled

Dreamlike into a painting a painting and slid back out of it
Like a wet horse, but in it no fault, either or away, no,

I know. Still life with you, away. A river can plead, it can;
You lied about this too and I remember it, remember you

Going out into the empty fields. You cannot leave a place
If you know where you are going. No why, but since,

Either it. Well then. Ambled dreamlike along and out,
A blue dismantling, breaking bottles on the bedside as you

Went, the cold so sharp it felt arranged. In circles. On the hills.
I want you to feel this but know nothing, I do not want

You to know I want you to feel. To *feel it*. Stop. Out. So
What. I can bear it but not for long, I do not encourage

Courage, that is the last thing I encourage. A broken door
Handle, the audio of the shipwreck buried also, in that house,

A crypt with any pleasure gouged out of it and sewn shut.
I remember it differently. So I bring it back a different way.

I remember what lies sweetly on a picture, what runs off,
What glances back. If I wait for you I will do it out here,

Drinking this lemony backwater. I will stay in these clothes.

Plates and furniture were broken, it happened
It happened. To be believed I had to make

My days measurable, and since doubt is an
Open fling, here is what was conclusive: a man

I did not know, shaking the morning out
Like an ice-tray; that this came first, and then

The next, and then. As if the damage could be
Scraped off so easily, as if a report so crisply

Linear could be so flawed, a memory folding
Through the blood in green sheets. The water

At that hour was not like water, the sentences
Uncertain, the beasts wild; but there, then,

In that terrible gulping cavern, I let you in
On a secret: *I never believed you*. And I have been

The same now for a long time. I've no love left
For secrecy, the wicked fucking *work* of it –

Doubt is an open fling, a wet riddle, a dark
Cloud dark cloud, happened it happened:

That fingers were crushed into wood and memory
Blocked up in my pores like cubes of salt.

That the rain is now, glass curtains of it.

Coming home late from a stoning,
Putting your coat up on the rack,

Making coffee. Closing the door.
What were you saying, something

About parallax; colours as vibrations,
As distances that collect pain, as ways

To put back together. What was taken.
Apart. Step backwards until you see it,

Until the lines join: the secret's perilous
Sway between failure (known) and

Success (not-known but not known to
Be not-known). And lastly, the facts:

You said you never would but you did.
You always said there wasn't but there was.

You said you said it but you had not.
By the time I say this I will have said it.

And why would I say something twice.
If something is true how do you wash it

Away. How do you know if something
Is true until you have washed it away.

We said we said it but did we, did we.

And are the nudes, at the same time, closely related to the appearance of specific people? Are they to some extent portraits of bodies?

Well,

                      I've known

the contours

                    grafted

onto

                    that particular

         question

           form

is

     a continuously floating

                  , of course,

difficulty

Whether Mortal Men May Attain True Happiness

I bite ice-cream with my
        front teeth & collect badly
bound books because danger
    I adore you   still I
wait for the dark it will hit
me like being struck around
the face with an Alaskan
king salmon   how each
frothy bursting planet
        rolls around the other &
such gracious witchery does
            not cease not
                even in death
how alive now feel each
    of my sordid procedures
how romantic to hold my
body in such a way as this
    pray give me time at least to tidy
away my unextraordinary things
            before you crank me
        open like a fabulous oyster like
the larynx of HE   I pick at Him
like a scab   a yellowed
edition of *City of God* comes
apart in my hands
            snaps like I meant
        nothing to it   raspberry coconut
burn me

Death Poem

I dreamed I was on a pier with Ingmar Bergman,
We must have been in one of the early films
As everything was black and white.

He was irritable because I was
Bothering him with questions and he was doing something
With rope and tools.

What are your films about?
I asked. He sighed
And put the tools down. TIME, he said,

And pay attention to the water.
But I don't remember any water in *Wild Strawberries* (1957), I said,
And only the beach scene in *The Seventh Seal* (1957).

Then you weren't watching closely, he said, and besides,
I've more films than that. He went back to his work.
Later, as he tied those great black knots, he said:

Watch the way the water behaves. You'll see
What they are about; seeing each other,
How you see through things, reflection. Ah!

I said, so they are about more
Than just TIME! Well, he said, looking out at the sea,
Perhaps you have got me there.

Aubade

for M

Inside me there is a
streak of you like
there is in the earth
a mirror. Any time,
whenever, it's ok,
you can come over.
Love is in my life,
hand by hand, visible.

This Mysterious

for Lawrie

Enter by night the moon moon moon
slipping down through the smart
hatch of your gaze – watching

as the cold truth of it ties a cat's-
cradle between your fingers. Little
wutherer, I wish for you huge

luminous, scribbles and stridency,
boiled milk – to be as
wakingly baffled as any of us

who float this mysterious
glass canoe over
the numberless goings-on of life

all you can hold. All you can hold.
And yes life can be held.
And yes I do fear.

But unhooked chunks of
night flocking to your side
like great-aunts come through

the sonic cold, bearing fruit
and feeble explanations for
everything, not least the gravity

that hangs – speechless –
from your thumb. Go,
in your small wellies

across the endless rooftops

Mary and the Angel

I returned to the place and when I passed it was raining,
Stopping to regard the house across the road
In a long coat like a spy or lost lover, when the family

Who lives there now pulled up and piled in and I was
Laughing, laughing at this hurt I had shaped for myself,
Thinking what dreadful movie I perform in as I stepped away,

Cut off from the flickers of life which once had slept in me,
Watching bow from the clouds a new absurdity to be lived with,
A bright and alert and ridiculous space between us.

Landscape

God said

freely I put you day by day this creation without a name

I said
I will put some stones
in a landscape

and I will call it *Stone Landscape*

or *Landscape with Stones*

with varying degrees of physical and moral authority I did
tend my stones

all the time I suspected someone
was there

at the edge of some vast anger

my life was like
a tree He
could float
to the top of

look, I said

and I took
two stones that were near and held them up

and God

beaming

took them from me

Iafnlengd

Where have you been, where are you, stay
　　Indoors tonight. You can't tell behind your
Herb-stuffed sleepmask but the design

　　Of the streets & gardens has gone awry. *Rock-
A-bye-baby*— you sleep well but yr sheep howl
　　& suffer in the lightning-scaffolded fields.

Cast off, no-one is too lonely at sea. *In the tree
　　Top*— to sleep is to give up, *when the wind blows* back
To sleep: infinitive. Exclamation. Command.

　　As clockwork, *the cradle will rock* & you
Are putting yr fist through glass to sleep, to sleep,
　　You are scarred with yr starting. Come, come,

You're lifeless like porcelain & sudden as toothache.
　　When the bough breaks the cradle
Delirious breathless potent *will fall*. Fingers

　　As cotton & eggshell, branches as unanchored
& serious beings. *& down will come baby*.
　　I do you wrong to take you out o the bed— you,

Unguarded somnambulant among the brass & fineries
　　Tentatively lifting & dropping yr name
Like feathers, like a confession, *cradle & all*—

Victorine

Le Déjeuner sur l'herbe, 1863

the eyes are not the mirror
of the soul   look
into my interminable
          mouth if you want to learn
something about dirt
               I was smug as a puddle
     having learnt all the elements
& how to fly a kite
               & why would I
have put back on my hazardous
blue dress when I could
be as cold as a fisherman
awkward as an ankle
     when I could show off my
glamorous toes & kneecaps
          not me I'll spit out
the disgrace & drink it
back   fuck it's hard being
nice all the time   but it is
good to fly a kite
          it is good to lie down
where the ground has come
          through & feel it
     closely   to become so
many flowers felt
     down the spine   whisper
to the men on either side
of me until they
          believe   *if my name*
were not a noun it would be
               a beautiful verb

And So We Invented The Wheel

and still we were afraid
of everything we
had not created.

And when we were done
what was left of
the trees still delivered the wind,

warmed themselves by living in their little flings.
They were still singing my heart,
that filthy project.

On deleting a villanelle about my grandfather

Boulevard Montmartre, Effet de nuit, 1897

Looking down to waxy traffic, it is all I can do

to not weep like an
old, brass coin. And outside

the night
lying down
like a glove   and your astonishment

of hands, healing here
            in this soft hotel.

     And you –
the willowy streetlamp
I put my hands to

O

dear moon i have forgotten your name again , forgive me .
o ragged dreamcatcher moon , o empty theatre moon .   it is cold
down here i cant feel my fingers .   dear moon i am drunk on light
and thinking about how churches look after dark .   do you
ever feel distracted by the sunset ?   it is very cold .   o
toothache moon o chessboard moon , drive me home .   dear moon
down here it is exciting to go to bed with your shoes on
and sometimes i wonder if im only biting my tongue to stop you
from hearing my teeth chattering .   moon i have never sold my body
for less than it was worth .   down here it is easy to forget
about ecstasy .   o wet underbelly of moon covered in twigs
from sleeping in the hedges , you are a heaven waiting to be poured
out .   i have written this in condensation , i hope thats ok .   you
were never one for mementos .   down here everything is fine .
o silver foil moon .   o vulnerable , triumphant moon .
o locked bathroom cabinet of moon it is ok to make mistakes .
i hate to see you sat huddled under the window like that ,
wont you come back to bed .   im sorry to say most nights
i can hear you talking to yourself , dont worry .   dear moon
i am scared about everything too .   o old cabbage moon
from down here you look as smooth as an oboe but i know
you have secrets .   i know the rooms within a scar .   o dearest
moon , i love the nights like these .   the sky gets so complicated .
its nights like these that make me wish i could do your cold job
for you .   keeping the sky upright , washing the heavy hills.

*When the braine is sore shaken, speach
is taken away*

Notes

"I Fear Thunder & Lightning...": The title of this poem is taken from Matthew Paris, the 13th-century chronicler, who says that Henry III, out of fear, ordered his royal barge to dock at the residence of the Bishop of Durham after a thunderstorm began. Simon de Montfort was lodging there and came to comfort Henry. Henry, supposedly, said these words to him.

"Enemy of the People": The epigraph of this poem is one of the many fictionalised versions of what Henry II said in reference to Archbishop of Canterbury Thomas Becket, leading to his murder by individuals who believed they were acting on the king's direct orders.

"Ape of Form": The title of this poem is from *Love's Labour's Lost*:

> BIRON   why, this is he
> That kiss'd his hand away in courtesy;
> This is the ape of form, monsieur the nice,
> That, when he plays at tables, chides the dice
> In honourable terms...

"What is the wind, what is it": A question posed by Gertrude Stein in *Tender Buttons* (1914).

"A motorway is a very strong wind": The title of this poem is taken from Yorgos Lanthimos's film *Dogtooth* (2009).

"And are the nudes...": An erasure of an interview of Francis Bacon conducted by David Sylvester.

"Whether Mortal Men May Attain True Happiness": A chapter title in St. Augustine's *The City of God*.

"Mary and the Angel": Inspired in part by one of Fra Angelico's depictions of the Annunciation – not the better-known one in the Prado, but the one in the Museo Nazionale di San Marco. Thanks to Celia for talking to me about the real subject of this painting.

"Iafnlengd": *Even-length*; the equinox.

The italics on page 8 and 35 are from a surgical textbook by William Clowes published in 1588. The full title is: *A prooued practise for all young chirurgians, concerning burnings with gunpowder, and woundes made with gunshot, sword, halbard, pyke, launce, or such other Wherein, is deliuered with all faithfulnesse, not onely the true receipts of such medicines as shall make them bolde, but also sundry familiar examples, such, as may leade them as it were by the hand, to the doyng of the lyke. Heereto is adioyned a treatise of the French or Spanish pockes, written by Iohn Almenar, a Spanish physition. Also, a commodious collection of aphorismes both English and Latin, taken out of an old written coppy. Published for the benefyte of his countrey, by Wylliam Clowes, mayster in chirurgery. Seene, and allowed, according to the order appoynted.*

The engraving on the final page is Emblem 189 in Andrea Alciato's *Emblemata* (1621).

Acknowledgements

Many thanks to the editors of the magazines and journals in which some of these poems first appeared: *14 poems*, *amberflora*, *Anthropocene*, *bathmagg*, *Blackbox Manifold*, *For Every Year*, *Pain*, *PERVERSE*, *Poetry London*, *The Scores*, *Stand*, and *Zarf*.

Thanks, also, to those who have edited these poems in their earlier forms or offered other invaluable forms of support and encouragement: The Society of Authors, Christ Church Oxford, Girton College Cambridge, Simon Armitage, Jack Belloli, Olivia Bradley, Anna Camilleri, Vahni Capildeo, Mary Anne Clark, Dave Coates, Tom Cook, Sarah Fletcher, Annie Hayter, Kai Jenkins, Bhanu Kapil, Zaffar Kunial, Adam Leonard, Helen Mort, Jeremy Noel-Tod, Flora Pery-Knox-Gore, Camille Ralphs, Richard Scott, Annabel Sim, Ben Sims, Phoebe Stuckes, Rebecca Tamás, Jonny Wiles, and countless others whose names escape me.

Thank you, Aaron, for your time, patience and trust.

Thank you, Adam – this book is your fault.

Dramatis Personae

Chorus of those who have seen the light played by those who have not
Oracle, or similarly oracular being
Lovers
Thin and open sheaves of light, sparsely so
Inconsolata (various)
Prayers, licked with hot applause
Those who have not
Dancers
Raincloud
Raincloud my hymnal

LAY OUT YOUR UNREST

Lightning Source UK Ltd.
Milton Keynes UK
UKHW022105271021
392955UK00005B/82

"Dirt is deliberate about the marrow of us. Performing vivisections of the body, trepanning the soul, Dominic Leonard's poems are subtle, aching instigators of curious joy. Here, the poet clears a febrile space in the world's anthropocene, and its antiquity, flooding the basin of regretful human appetite with a hoard of honeyed sound, showing how we inhabit "a bright and alert and ridiculous space between us." Allow yourself the cadence of these poems' heartbreak, their incandescing of the everyday, their mining of the spirit to its broken back teeth: they may not comfort, overmuch, but that is their sublime magic."
— *Shivanee Ramlochan*

Dominic Leonard's poems and sequences, as delicate-seeming as the breathing mechanism of some rare animal, are moving and courageous: Dirt knows the kinship of hesitancy, doubt and error with passion and truth, as do its influences, from Emily Sickinson to medieval mystery plays."
—*Vahni Capildeo*

Dominic Leonard's *Dirt* is a dark and windswept collection as mysterious as the mist hovering over a mountain. Leonard's deep interest in language shows in his fascination with pre-medieval poetry and drama, while his writing bears the fruit of the full bloodline of English literature, from Chaucer to Shakespeare, from Keats to T.S. Eliot. Essentially a romantic figure, Leonard is a young man with an old soul "Carving his mouth open....To get out all the slush, all the necessary dirt."

UK: £7.99 / US: $10.99 / EUR €9.99

ISBN 978-1-913642-72-3

Broken Sleep Books

lay out your unrest

9 781913 642723 >